Faithbuilders Publishing

Fragrance of Faith

by Doreen Harrison

Fragrance of Faith by Doreen Harrison

First Published in Great Britain in 2017

FAITHBUILDERS PUBLISHING www.biblestudiesonline.org.uk

An Imprint of Apostolos Publishing Ltd,

3rd Floor, 207 Regent Street,

London W1B 3HH

www.apostolos-publishing.com

Copyright © 2016 Doreen Harrison

All rights reserved. No part of this book may be reproduced or transmitted in any form or by any means, electronic or mechanical, including photocopying, recording, or by any information storage and retrieval system, without permission in writing from the publisher.

Unless otherwise indicated, all scripture quotations in this publication are from the Good News Translation in Today's English Version- Second Edition Copyright © 1992 by American Bible Society. Used by Permission.

Scripture quotations marked "ESV" are from The Holy Bible, English Standard Version, copyright ©2001 by Crossway Bibles, a publishing ministry of Good News Publishers. Used by permission. All rights reserved.

British Library Cataloguing-in-Publication Data

A catalogue record for this book is available from the British Library

ISBN: 978-1-912120-65-9

Cover Design by Blitz Media, Pontypool, Torfaen

Cover Image © | Dreamstime Stock Photos.

Other stock photo illustrations used under license and are credited throughout.

Printed and bound in Great Britain by Marston Book Services Limited, Oxfordshire.

Dedicated to all those who (like me) are of senior years.

By the same author: A Bouquet of Blessings, A Garland of Grace, The Donkey Boy, Jubilant Jeremy Johnson, Coping with the Wobbles of Life.

Contents

A Risk of Ice	8
The Green Coat	10
Ring That Bell!	12
Precious Memories?	14
God of All the Earth	16
Winter Leads to Spring!	18
Walking by Faith	20
The Dawn Chorus	22
Love and Cobbles	24
Communication	26
The Colour of Life	28
The Game of Life	30
Silent Spring?	32
Wonderfully Made!	34
No More Grey Hair?!	36
More than Easter Bunnies	38
China Cups	40
A-Maze-ing Grace	42
Queen of Contentment	44
Strawberry Moon	46
Pretty Primroses	48
Lasting Memories	50
Live and Let Live	52
Enjoy the Sunshine!	54
Enhance the Present	56

Big Thoughts	58
Blackberry Bushes	60
Status Quo Vadis?	62
Prayer Works	64
Falling Leaves	66
Battleship Banter!	68
The First Christmas	70
Happy Christmas Memories	72
Enjoy Today!	74
Celebration Cake!	76

This book is the third part of the trilogy, "A Bouquet of Blessings" with the other books being "A Bouquet if Blessings" and "A Garland of Grace." It contains anecdotes, stories, thoughts which will hold you together when situations and circumstances are causing you to fall apart. It is a book for a bedside table, a coffee table, for a birthday gift, for a sick friend. It will fit into an A5 envelope. There are blessings in its pages, gathered through a life of variety and events which all underline the truth that Jesus saves, keeps—and satisfies—always and for ever.

© Katarzyna Zwolska | Dreamstime.com

A Risk of Ice

A screen on our car dashboard obligingly informs us that there is a 'risk of ice', when the temperature drops to 3 degrees. We know then that the gritters will be moving in, and we walk and drive with caution, because, of course, ice is slippery.

We wear jumpers, hats, scarves, gloves, boots—and some particularly chilly people carry hot water bottles! And through it all, we do not doubt that if winter comes, spring is not far behind. Here in the UK, we take it for granted that that the promise God gave to Noah continues to be unbroken: *'As long as the world exists, there will be a time for planting and a time for harvest. There will always be cold and heat, summer and winter, day and night'.* Of course, there will—experience proves it and God has promised it.

The last leaves have blown off the trees, and we now appreciate the strength and structure of each trunk and branch, outlined against the wintery sky, with buds already identifying leaves to burst out next spring. Bulbs already push eager shoots through the soil, which will continue to develop undaunted by alien temperatures. Planet Earth will spin through the winter solstice, with mathematical precision, because it was set in motion by the Great Designer himself.

The eyes with which you are reading this are an amazing structure: your brain translates what you see and enables you to understand the message. We are fearfully and wonderfully made. Each time I hear, or read, of yet another erudite discourse on the vastness of space with universes beyond our own universe, I am amazed anew that we live safely on this spinning planet which revolves in space, without visible support, surrounded by blackness—and we take it all for granted!

Whenever I hear the song, 'He's got the whole world in His hands', I want to add an additional chorus, 'Thank goodness for that!' Indeed, the complete irrationality of the dependability of human existence on planet earth should awaken a deep - seated gratitude that God is in control.

The Green Coat

I recollect a lady who was referred for counselling, and on her first appointment she arrived wearing a heavy green coat, with a shawl collar—only remarkable because it was June, and the UK was experiencing a heat wave! Although there was a place to hang coats, she kept hers on. However, as the session continued, she began to perspire, and finally, she shrugged off the coat and sighed. 'That was my camouflage!' she confessed. This lady was anorexic, painfully thin, and she hid her problem under the heavy green coat.

I recollect this incident at the beginning of a new year. God asks us, 'What sort of camouflage are you wearing, my children?' With 365 unspoiled days ahead of us, it is vital that we step over the threshold on the new year without pretense or cover up. 'Here I am - wholly available,' should be our prayer—not who I was, nor who I would like to be, just me, just as I am.

Anorexia is usually due to a need to be in control. Often due to circumstances or situation, refusing to eat is the only self-control available. It is such a relief to remember that God is always in control. He is absolutely reliable at all times and in all places. We do not need to impress God with our own ability—or lack of ability! He welcomes us into His family when we let go of self, and sin, and let Him take over. His is an unconditional acceptance.

The day came when the lady no longer needed that heavy green coat—she no longer needed camouflage. She understood that God loved her and that His control was unthreatening and the she was free in His love and grace. She had transferred control to God. Consider these verses from the Bible:

'May you always be joyful in your union with the Lord. I say it again: rejoice! Show a gentle attitude toward everyone. The Lord is coming soon. Don't worry about anything, but in all your prayers ask God for what you need, always asking him with a thankful heart. And God's peace, which is far beyond human understanding, will keep your hearts and minds safe in union with Christ Jesus'. (Philippians 4:4–7)

May you know the joy of the Lord to be your strength all through the year ahead.

© Paul Maguire | Dreamstime.com

Ring That Bell!

I collect bells, and one which rings many memories for me is the school bell from the first school at which I taught. Soon after I started work, the bell was replaced by a whistle—because playground noise could frequently overwhelm the clanging of the bell, and the children did not, or chose not to (?!), notice the adult who wielded it, however furiously it rang.

When I left that school, the redundant bell was added to my collection. Imagine my surprise, then, when I read the news item which I now quote: 'A school has banned teachers from blowing a whistle to end playtime, in case it scares children. Instead, they must put up a hand and wait for the children to notice!' A whistle is thought to be too aggressive and some children might be afraid.

When I identify the variety of videos, computer games, TV series, and smart phone items, which even children under 5 years of age are exposed to, I find it hard to believe that a whistle blast, however shrill or loud, could frighten any one. Although, possibly a nonagenarian, who might associate a whistle with the pronouncement, 'Game over!' The article concluded with the statement; 'Last night the school had not responded with a request for comment.'

A whistle, blown by authority, proclaims a boundary. In the case of a school playground, it identifies the boundary between time out and time in. It is a secure sound, someone is in control, someone is responsible for what will happen next, someone is keeping watch over what is happening, someone is in charge.

Consider this encouraging whistle blast from the Bible:

'Do not be afraid—I am with you! I am your God—let nothing terrify you! I will make you strong and help you; I will protect you and save you …. The Lord who created you says, "Do not be afraid—I will save you. I have called you by name—you are mine'. (Isaiah 41:10; 43:1) And, of course, with the nonagenarian in mind, the final whistle for those who believe in God's mercy in Jesus Christ does not only indicate 'Game over.' It also indicates that a new game is about to begin. It proclaims time out of earth—but time to enter Heaven.

Precious Memories?

We have grown accustomed to pictures of long lines of refugees, tracking from country to country in search of security, with their entire previous history contained in bundles, sacks, and, of course, in the family who are with them. In decades to come what memories of childhood will these children retain? If we had to pack our previous lifestyle into one small bag, what would we choose to take with us? If we only had room or time to select one item, what would it be?

I thought long and carefully about this. Shall I opt for a special photo? Or something valuable, but easy to carry, which I could exchange for money to establish my future when the long walk was over? Or would it be a memento of an event which was a mile stone in my life before I began the long walk to freedom? Or might I choose a warm rug, a practical solution for a comfortless journey? I would need something to express hope, confidence that tomorrow could be better than today.

I decided that I would choose a small plaster bell, which would fit into my pocket; here is the reason for this choice. When my two daughters were small, we went on a day trip to the sea side.

Clutching little purses in which was their spending money, they gazed with amazement at the treasure trove in the shell and souvenir shops which lined the promenade. They noted the cascade of sweet rock novelties in the beach shops and the colorful buckets, spades, and flags ready to be used to embellish the expanse of sand with an enormous sand castle! What to buy?

Finally, decided, they went into one of the shops with their Dad—reappearing, excitedly, they presented me with a parcel; 'It's for you,' they explained. 'It cost all our money— but it's because we love you!' The extravagance of such love would certainly sustain me wherever the journey took me!

God so loved the world that He gave everything He had so that each of us could journey through life to a safe destination at its end. Jesus lived, died, and rose again. Faith in him gives hope whatever happens.

God of All the Earth

A ball is round—unless it is a rugby ball—and balls come in a variety of sizes; a beach ball, a tennis ball, the earth itself, which has a diameter at the equator of 24,901 miles!

There was a time when people believed that the earth was flat, and intrepid voyagers sailed with the uncertainty of finishing the journey by falling off its edge! Today, the earth is becoming a place of easy access. Modern technology can circle it in seconds with speech or even visually. The world hasn't changed in size or shape, but humanity has advanced in skill and science and because of this it is as if the world has 'shrunk' to a manageable size.

In my first teaching post, I was also the first person in the village to fly to America! On my return, I was greeted with awe and amazement! Nowadays we could fly to USA for a weekend, if we were inclined to do so. In one sense, then, the well - known lyric,

'He's got the whole wide world in His hands' has become more credible. Our concept of the world has changed. An Almighty, omnipresent, omniscient God might indeed hold this planet in His hands, just as easily as you or I can hold a ping pong ball! Of course, this does depend on the size of the God in whom we believe!

I write during a week of EU Referendum frenzy, and the fact that God is in control is most reassuring The Bible gives us emphatic advice:

'First of all, then, I urge that petitions, prayers, requests, and thanksgivings be offered to God for all people; for kings and all others who are in authority, that we may live a quiet and peaceful life with all reverence toward God and with proper conduct.' (1 Tim 2:1–2)

If you have carefully considered both sides of the argument, to exit or to stay, well done! But if you consider applying to God for His assessment of the situation - you will have done even better! Persistent prayer can overwhelm political power. Am I 100% sure of this? Why not make it 24,901%?

Winter Leads to Spring!

A newspaper featured a delectable photograph of a field in Cornwall, full of a spring splendor of daffodils on the 15th of January. At the side of the photograph was an ominous warning: 'Arctic blasts to bring sleet, snow and danger! The higher than average temperatures of recent months are likely to come to an abrupt end!' Such is life. We read that councils are well prepared for the cold conditions, having stock piled 1.2 million tons of salt to keep traffic moving—although drivers have been told to expect problems.

However, if winter comes, can spring be far behind? If a situation deteriorates, one option is that things can only get better! Tomorrow is another day. This last phrase reminds me of a Yorkshire shepherd, whose daily task was to walk round Little Whernside, checking up on his flock. I asked him, 'Do you need to do that every day?' He replied with surprise in his voice, 'Oh yes. They are my responsibility.' He was there, sun, rain, snow, yesterday, today, and tomorrow; a veteran of care and compassion. He was a good shepherd.

I heard of an old shepherd who was moving his sheep into another field. As he opened the gate to let them through, he slipped and fell. The entire flock trampled over him to reach their new pasture. Painfully he got to his feet and closed the gate. Later he explained, 'It's all part of the job.' He quoted the Bible: *'The good shepherd lays down his life for the sheep.'* (John 10:11 ESV)

When circumstances change and the storms of life cover what was bright and beautiful, just like the snow showers could obliterate the daffodils in Cornwall, remember that life still goes on and tomorrow will be different. God, our Shepherd, is never taken by surprise and He is with us, always. Another Bible verse declares, *'the Lord is my shepherd, I shall not want.'* (Psalm 23:1 ESV)

God has already prepared for every eventuality.

Walking by Faith

I discovered an intriguing cartoon, which depicted a man, shuffling along with his feet encased in two large jars of Vick! Intrigued, I read the accompanying article. Apparently, some people have 'discovered' that Vick, rubbed onto the soles of your feet, is more effective than Vick rubbed on to your chest. The final sentence advised: 'If you do this at night, wear socks to protect the bed clothes!' I hesitate to confirm the benefit of walking with Vick!

There is a verse in Ephesians chapter 6 which describes the whole armour of God: 'Have your feet fitted with the readiness that comes from the gospel of peace.' It is possible that Vick on the feet might enable you to breathe deeply and strongly. Fitted out with faith presents the wearer with that breath of life with which we can, 'Rejoice in the Lord always.' Then our gentleness will be evident to all, anxiety will dissolve away and the peace of God—which transcends all understanding—will guard our hearts and minds in Christ Jesus. With hallelujahs, I extol the blessing of walking in faith!

A cartoon is designed to make you laugh. It is unfortunate that often the way we Christians shuffle through life is more of a joke than a jubilant fact. Consider this verse from Isaiah chapter 52:

'How beautiful on the mountains are the feet of those who bring good news, who proclaim peace, who bring good tidings and proclaim salvation, who say to Zion, Your God reigns.' May we all determine to walk in victory - for the glory of God.

> *When we walk with the Lord, in the light of His word*
> *What a glory He sheds on our way.*
> *While we do His good will, He abides with us still -*
> *And with all who will trust and obey.*
> (Hymn by John H. Sammis, 1887)

© Vladvitek | Dreamstime.com

The Dawn Chorus

In spite of a frosty mist which hides the mountains, the birds are beginning to sing their dawn chorus—although maybe the late arrival of dawn is an encouragement to the feathered choir? But there is no doubt that spring is about to burst into this winter weary world. We can count as a blessing that at 5 pm now there is still light in the sky! There are no snow drifts, no flu epidemic, no national disaster, and no diminishing of God's grace. Every dark night gives way to a new day, and there is likelihood that tomorrow will be better than today.

We live in an amazing generation. We take for granted central heating, washing machines, tumble dryers, fridge, freezers, microwaves, television, mobile phones, computers, Facebook, and the ability to speak and Skype with people at the other side of the world. We accept air travel, space travel, and take for granted incredible medical care.

I noted a grisly headline in a newspaper which announced, 'Monkey head transplant ready for humans!' Cautiously I read on. 'A monkey has received a head transplant using a controversial technique that is almost ready to be tried on humans, scientists have claimed.' Truly controversial, although the technique does not intend to place a chimpanzee head on Mr. Jones! It is important that we read with care and do not jump to conclusions.

In the Bible there are 823,156 words (King James version). The 35th word introduces this sentence: *'God said "Let there be light - and there was light."'* It is an undeniable fact that light overcomes darkness, that in our world there is light.

At the bottom of Big Pit, a former coal mine in Blaenavon (now a working museum), the darkness is impenetrable. But light just one little match and the darkness retreats. However deep, dark, discouraging the situation might be—the smallest faith can begin to diminish the darkness. The blessing which we must not ignore concerns the undeserved grace of God.

Consider this ancient prayer: *'Lighten our darkness we beseech thee, O Lord, and by Thy great mercy, defend us from all perils and dangers of this night, for the love of Thine only Son, our Saviour, Jesus Christ.'*

Love and Cobbles

The next few weeks are characterized by love. Valentine's Day is ushered in with a plethora of roses and red hearts. Now the stores are overwhelming, with ways in which to purchase and present 'I love my Mum.'

Then it is Easter, with Easter eggs and hot cross buns which symbolize the love which is indestructible, that love of God in Christ Jesus which burst through death—and Jesus, now, is alive for ever more.

I am reminded of a family love story which I first heard many years ago from my Grandmother. My great, great, great Grandmother (!) was called Katie Wheelan, and she came from Ireland to work in a Yorkshire woolen mill. With her curly hair, dimpled cheeks, and delicious sense of humor, she won the heart of the mill owner's son, James, and he asked her to marry him. 'Come up to my home, meet my parents,' he said.

Katie had no special clothes, but she was neat and tidy, as she made her way up the long drive to the big house. She rang the bell. A maid, in uniform, opened the door. She looked disdainfully at the humble mill girl. 'Your place is at the back door, at the servants' entrance,' she told Katie, who explained, 'But Master James is expecting me!' James's mother came to see what was happening. 'And who are you?' she asked. James was there as well. He came out and took Katie's hand. 'Mother' he said, 'This is Katie, the girl I intend to marry.' There was a long silence. Then James's mother spoke. 'This is a mill girl and one day you will own the mill. She is not suitable for you—you must choose between us and her!'

"Then I choose Katie!' said James. And he did! He left home and married Katie and they really did live happily ever after. James worked on the roads. He became a 'setter', setting cobbles in place so that horses could draw their burdens in safety, so that travelers could move easily from place to place. I think his new job was appropriate to the choice he made.

Love makes life's journey secure and safe. Consider these words from the Bible 'What does the Lord require of you? To act justly, and to love mercy and to walk humbly with your God.'

Communication

Possibly one of the down-sides of Facebook or Twitter is that they might diminish the art of conversation! Statements are made, opinions are given online, but genuine conversation consists of personality reacting with personality and words used in conversation are enhanced by tone, inflexion, volume, and body language; all of which emphasize the meaning.

Consider the simple phrase, 'Go away!' Accompanied with a loud voice, a stamp of the foot, a frown, those two words have a completely different meaning than if they were spoken with a laugh and raised eyebrows, implying 'You don't expect me to believe THAT, surely!'

I recall an occasion when a distraught neighbor came around to share sad news. I offered comforting words but someone else who was there had the common sense to put the kettle on and provide a cup of hot, sweet, sustaining tea. Sometimes actions speak louder than words—often both words and actions are necessary.

My granddaughter does work experience in a residential home. She tells me that some elderly people don't seem to understand her when she talks to them, but if she sits beside them and gently strokes their hands, they usually smile and often begin to hum quietly—or even sing.

Body language of a different kind is revealed at various borders, where the crowds of refugees are faced with barricades which reinforce the words, 'Go away! We don't want you here!' However, even in the former Calais 'Jungle' there was a group called *Youth with a Mission*, who manned a feeding station and provide numerous cups of tea to a multitude of people whose language is different to theirs—but who understood the body language of compassion and concern.

The Bible explains that *'The Word was made flesh and lived among us, and we saw his glory'*. The kindness of God was expressed in the body language of His son Jesus, who reinforced God's word by the way he lived, died, and rose again. His words and actions, his body language, proclaimed a resounding 'Go away' to fear, despair, worry, and sin!

The Colour of Life

We celebrated a family birthday in a Bristol restaurant which served delicious food, but specialized in exotic fruit juices, served in tall glasses, with twisty straws and paper parasols to match the colour of the fruit. Banana, mango, and passion fruit were decorated with lemon parasols, strawberry juice sported pretty pink. My granddaughter collected all the parasols and stuck them in her hair. Delightful! I remembered a group of children in Africa who came to a celebration and they had adorned their tight curly hair with little red flowers, a blossom for each twirl, thus making a cap of fragrant frivolity which readily matched their happy smiles. Someone remarked, 'See how they are beautifying their minds!'

The Bible gives good advice: *'Whatever is lovely, … think about these things.'* In the confused society, what these 'lovely things' are can be difficult to discern. There is so much division, despair, disarray, dismay, and distrust, that the newscasters run out of space for any brighter items.

The front page of our local paper was encouraging—the banner headline 'WORRIED!', concerning the proposed opening of an open cast mine near our home was accompanied, at the side, by an offer of Freesia bulbs, with a pretty posy picture to enhance it. But who noticed that lovely picture?

I watched a TV programme concerning a huge refugee camp which had expanded for many years across an arid, colourless, flat area—but there were lines of bright green bushes lining some of the featureless streets of grey tents: a lovely reminder that there is always some way in which a situation can be improved.

I once met a lady, very crippled and tired, who had painted her walking stick in red and white stripes so that it looked like a stick of candy!

The Bible declares, *'Whatever is true, whatever is honorable, whatever is just, whatever is pure, whatever is lovely, whatever is commendable, if there is any excellence, if there is anything worthy of praise, think about these things.'* (Phil 4:8 ESV)

This is the way to 'beautify our minds!' The choice is ours—consider another verse from the Bible: *'Seek and you WILL find'.* Look for loveliness today—it is surely there!

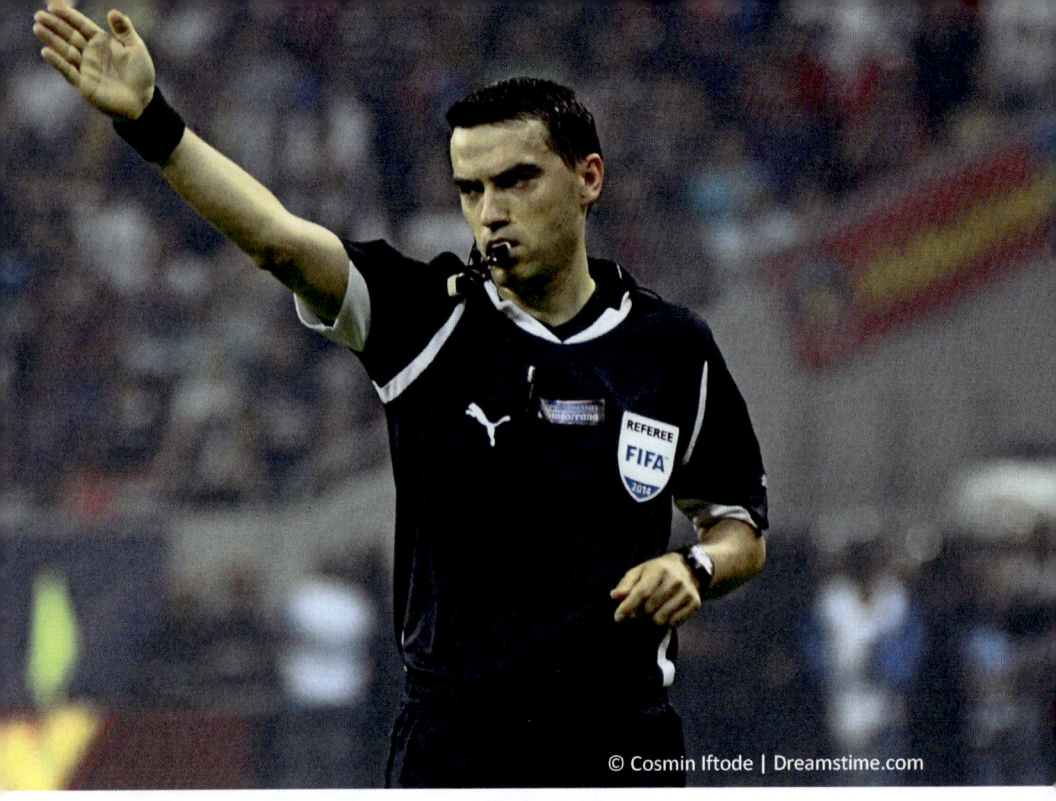

The Game of Life

I became a Christian on Palm Sunday, many years ago. The Preacher who led me to Christ said, 'When you accept Jesus as your Saviour and Lord, you will never be lonely again.' I have proved, since then, that Jesus's promise, *'And I will be with you always, to the end of the age'* (Matt 28:20) is incredibly true. I am so grateful that I joined His team.

A recent commentary on a particularly exciting rugby game described the team who won in two ways. He said, 'The team are fragile!' and later, 'This is a solid team!' Those of us who play life's game by heavenly rules declare, with St Paul, *'I really do not think that I have already won it; the one thing I do, however, is to forget what is behind me and do my best to reach what is ahead. So I run straight toward the goal in order to win the prize, which is God's call through Christ Jesus to the life above.'* (Phil 3:13–14)

But life can be tough and often we feel fragile. Then we remember the encouragement of words in Philippians chapter 4, *'I can do all things through Christ who gives me strength.'*

And we belong to a team; other Christians who are with us in this game of life. We are in this together. We are a partnership, being confident of this, *'God, who began this good work in you, will carry it on until it is finished on the Day of Christ Jesus'* (Phil 1:6). We are expected to be solid in our faith! Consider these words in 1 Peter 5:7–8, *'Leave all your worries with him, because he cares for you. Be alert, be on watch! Your enemy, the Devil, roams around like a roaring lion, looking for someone to devour. [9] Be firm in your faith and resist him*

The game is not over until the final whistle blows. However, this game has already been won! On Easter day, Jesus rose from the dead and lives for evermore. He is the captain of our Salvation and one day we shall see Him. Until then - we play our game according to His rules, set out in the Bible.

I can offer you three suggestions for a successful game. First—study the rule book. Second—respect the rest of the team. Third, and most important—obey your captain! Then you will understand the description given to Christians: we have ABUNDANT life!

Ours is definitely an exciting game. Care to join the team?

© Brian Lambert | Dreamstime.com

Silent Spring?

A recent broadcast really made me sit up and listen! The speaker was concerned about the silence of his bird table! He was describing how the birds still came to sample his selection of seeds and peanuts but they did not sing. He said that the blackbirds in his garden were less vocal than they used to be and he was thoughtful concerning the dawn chorus which delights us in early May; would that be silent as well?

Years ago, a book was written entitled 'Silent Spring'. The author predicted that pesticides, different farming methods, traffic pollution could decimate the bird population and empty our skies of bird flight and bird song. Certainly, the bird population is declining. The RSPB present a variety of reasons why this is happening - maybe our children will never see the abundance of bird life which we enjoyed?

I once taught in a school which was on the migratory route of house martins. I remember my first spring there. One morning, suddenly, a large flock of house martins landed in the school field, outside my classroom. There must have been a thousand of them. Awestruck, the children clustered around the window, no one spoke, but the sheer delight on their faces spoke louder than words!

Five minutes later, the whole flock rose and soared into the sky. Later still, the school caretaker told me, 'They come here every spring. Ever since I was little. This is their resting place near the end of the long journey.' I wonder if they still come?

An old country man, looking up at an evening sky patterned with birds flying back to roost, said, 'They write the music of creation against the clouds.' Indeed, the black flight against a rosy sunset did look like a musical score. When we sing, 'All things bright and beautiful - the Lord God made them all' we would be wise to remember that we hold planet earth on trust from God. Consider these lines from a well-known hymn: *'Change and decay in all around I see! O Thou who changest not, abide with me.'* (Henry Francis Lyte, 1861)

Songs of joy can come from human throats as well as from birds!! The unchanging message of Easter deserves the loudest Hallelujah we can muster. Things may change - but Jesus? Never! Glory to His name.

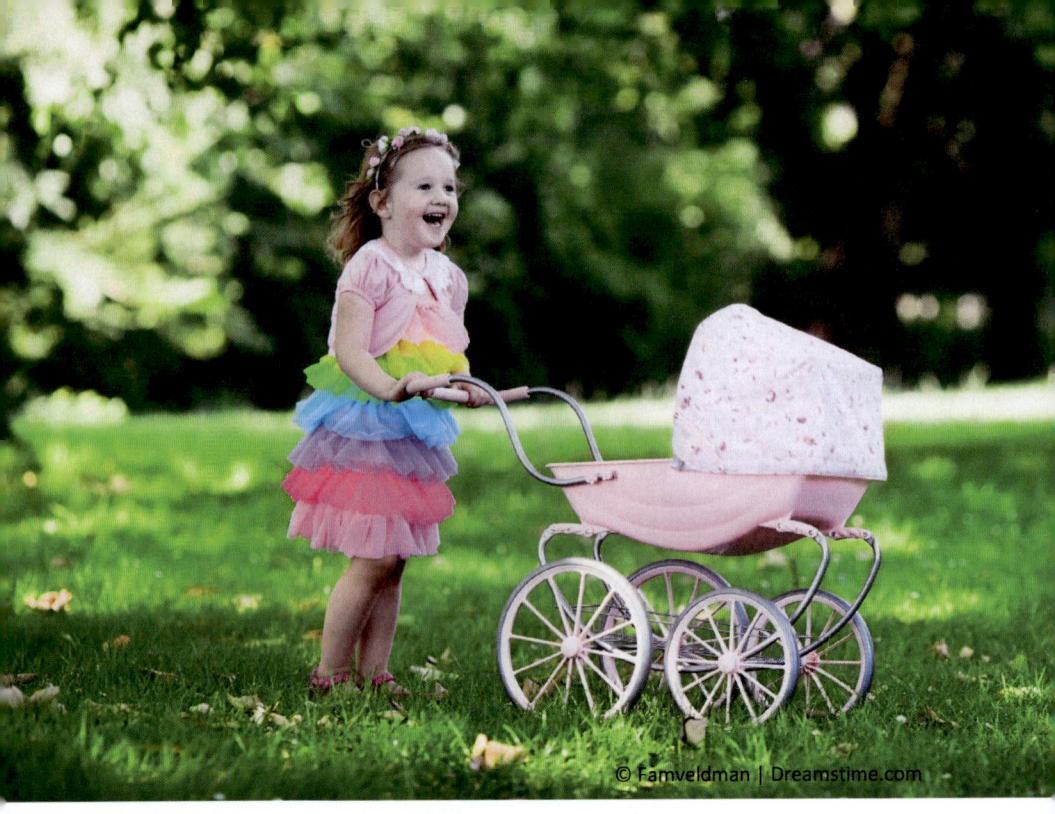

Wonderfully Made!

There was the pram and there was the baby! I assumed that the person pushing the pram was an older sister. My assumption was wrong! I bent down to look at the sweet little child and realized that I was cooing over a doll. It looked completely lifelike, with artificial skin that felt like flesh!

I recollected a recent item on the Internet. In a Tokyo department store a robot was confused for a human being. I quote: 'I wondered why on earth all these people were taking a picture of a receptionist? I looked at her carefully and then I realized it was a robot! The humanoids name is Aika Chihira. She is working in customer services and wears a silk kimono. She is 5 feet 5 inches high and powered by 43 motors. Her movements are finely tuned by a computer which transfers data at 30 times per second. The head of the team who made her stated, "The trick of getting a robot to look human is a difficult task. 80%

human like is very scary. So it has to be 90% or very close to perfect."'

The doll and the robot looked human but they were just clever replicas of the complex, complicated, and comprehensive combination which conforms human life.

The Bible comments *'I am fearfully and wonderfully made. Wonderful are your works'*. (Ps 139:14 ESV)

When God intruded into planet earth in the person of Jesus, He was not dealing with replicas. Jesus is 100% real! He was a real human baby, he grew up as a member of a human family, he learned a trade and worked as a carpenter, and he died - as do all human beings.

But because Jesus is the Son of God, he came back to life and at Easter we celebrate that awesome event. Our celebrations might include the Easter bunny, Easter eggs, daffodils, special food, spring sunshine, holiday time—but the real reason for the season is that we are celebrating the facts of faith.

God loves us, he came to save us, and he lives in the hearts and minds of those of us who investigate the reality of the Easter message.

No More Grey Hair?!

A national newspaper featured the usual dire headlines on its front page, but there was also a smaller headline which announced: 'End of grey hair in sight with gene discovery!' Scientists have isolated the gene which determines hair colour.

Does this also imply an end to wrinkles and other attributes of old age—and might it add unfortunate approval to a possible raising of retirement age to 70 years or even older? Is age defined by how we look, or how we feel? An accompanying article to the headline contained this delightful opinion: 'I'm proud of the family silver! I am grey and proud to be so. It is just beautiful!' This was written by a health and nutrition expert who has gone grey in her early 20s. Consider these two proverbs: *'Grey hair is a glorious crown,'* and *'We admire the strength of youth and respect the gray hair of age.'* (Prov 16:31; 20:29)

Maybe the cruel, chronic disability that sometimes accompanies old age is like a chrysalis case; inside the unyielding case is the beautiful potential of a gorgeous butterfly. Arthritic Granddad, leaning on his Zimmer, is still— inside—the young energetic man who even thought of climbing Mount Everest one day!

Grey hair is believed to be determined, 30 % by genes, and the rest by environmental factors. The genetic factor is being carefully investigated by experts. Environmental factors include what we eat (beware of sugar!); what we breathe (watch out for diesel!); what we believe (education matters, and so does faith!); and, of course, how long we have been alive!

Arthritic Granddad needs his Zimmer. He looks old but please do not assume that he feels old! The splendor attributed to grey hair is surely a combination of experience, memory, and contentment with situations which we cannot change. The Bible reminds us, *'I have learned in whatever situation I am to be content.'* (Phil 4:11) Whether we are young, old or in between— brunette, blonde or bald—we can rejoice in the splendor of this promise; God says, *'even to your old age I am he, and to gray hairs I will carry you. I have made, and I will bear; I will carry and will save.'* (Isa 46:4 ESV)

More than Easter Bunnies

I noted, with amusement, that a certain pet shop was not selling rabbits at Easter, out of deference to the Easter Bunny! Enjoy your Easter holiday, but please join me in identifying the real reason for this season of rejoicing. This is what happened on the first Easter day, 2000 years ago.

Very early in the morning, when grey mist coiled around the trunks of trees and the air still held the chill of night, a group of women hurried along the road to the garden. They carried spices to anoint the body of Jesus, who had been crucified two days before and hurriedly put into a tomb cave in a garden, to avoid desecrating the Jewish Sabbath. Grief plays tricks with memory and they had forgotten that the cave had been sealed with a large and heavy stone.

The sky held a collection of small lemon clouds, bouncing along the horizon as if the waiting sun was pushing them out of the way to make room for a new day. The garden gate was open, and as they stepped inside they became aware of a light which did not come from the sky, where now the lemon cloudlets were filling the horizon and the rim of the sun was showing over the top of the hills.

This light was richer! It came from the cave. It shone from inside the cave and that large stone had been rolled to one side! What had happened? As they stood there, puzzled and afraid, suddenly two men dressed in dazzling white stood beside them. The women bowed their faces to the ground, this light was too strong for them to bear. And, as they looked at the dewy wet grass, they knew what the two men were about to tell them.

For there, in the wet grass, were the marks of His footsteps, leading out of the tomb, back into life. 'He is not here. He has risen' announced the heavenly messengers. This is why we celebrate at Easter. Jesus rose from the dead - and He is alive for ever more.

China Cups

We were visiting a friend who now lives in a residential home. It was Monday afternoon and as we stepped into the spacious entrance hall, we noticed that it was set out with tables, covered with pretty cloths, and that the residents were sitting around the tables enjoying dainty cakes and tea in china cups! 'We always have afternoon tea on Monday,' explained one of the carers. Full marks to that residential home, for Monday afternoon tea memory time! For those elderly people, china cups and dainty cakes would be reminiscent of a previous generation when that sort of setting would allow them to feel special. The day of the dishwasher has led to the decline of china cups! However, there is an elegance in the appearance of china cups which dishwasher-proof mugs do not have. A steaming mug of hot tea, on a cold day or in a time of crisis is a marvelous comfort, but tea in a china cup can also be a soothing declaration that someone cares.

My attention was drawn to a photo of Marathon runners rushing past Buckingham Palace. The picture spoke louder than words! It showed the Palace, clearly defined, with the runners out of focus, to identify with their speed and the fact that they did not have time to stop—even if they were passing the Royal Palace and it was 'Her' birthday! They could not savor 'afternoon tea in china cups!', they had to get on with life!

Consider this story. A young woman got onto a crowded bus. No seat, but an elderly gentleman stood up, and with old world courtesy, offered her his seat. She dismissed him with a laugh. 'You need it more than I do, Granddad,' she said. The old gentleman had proffered a china cup of courtesy—but she made him feel a real old mug! It is important that we take care to consider other people; that we slow down and enjoy the world around us. Actually, that we notice the advice in the Bible and begin to 'Love our neighbor as much as we love ourselves.

The Bible announces that God considers each of us every day with special care. We read, *'How precious to me are your thoughts, O God! How vast is the sum of them! If I would count them, they are more than the sand.'* (Ps 139:17–18) Take time, today, to appreciate that incredible declaration.

A-Maze-ing Grace

We visited the Jubilee Maze at Symonds Yat. Planted in 1977 by 2 brothers, it presents a construction of paths from the entrance to the goal and the way out! It is constructed from over a kilometer of hedges. For thousands of years, on every continent, mazes have been made. The ancient mazes were designed to be 'serene and introspective,' and were created to send travelers on a spiritual journey. Over the centuries, mazes have become more intricate and complex.

In the 20th century, the earliest video games featured mazes! There is a viewing platform at the Jubilee maze from which the precise pattern of the paths can be appreciated - and instructions given to confused maze goers! I watched the family from this high aspect, and I also reached the goal before they did, because the owner of the maze showed me the direct route from there which is the only way out!

Life is like a maze. We enter at birth and through the years of living we travel along the twists and turns of situation and circumstances until we reach the end, which presents us with the only way out. However we define it, death is our decisive end. Over the centuries life has become more complex and intricate. Once, a man on the moon was as farcical as the myth that the moon is made of green cheese! The telephones were found in red kiosks on street corners. Flying across continents was the activity of migrating birds. Now, schoolchildren carry computers in their pockets—we take the amazing facility of a mobile phone for granted. There was a certain maze in which the proprietors had to issue maps, because so many people were using mobile phones to call the local police for help when they got lost in the maze

In life's maze, we are overseen by the Designer Himself. The Bible reassures us that God's eye is on each sparrow so He certainly regards you and me. We are provided with a detailed plan for our journey through life; the Bible is our handbook. These ancient truths are so that we will have a 'serene journey' and clearly identify the right way out!

Consider these words from Psalm 23 *'Surely goodness and mercy will follow me all the days of my life and I shall dwell in the house of the Lord forever.'* (Ps 23:6 ESV) And if we do get lost or take the wrong route, why not dial a prayer?

Queen of Contentment

At a belated celebration for her Majesty the Queen's 90th birthday, as we watched a DVD presentation of a recent garden party in Buckingham Palace grounds, someone commented that the Queens umbrella (yes, it was raining!), matched her lovely pink outfit. Came the reply, 'I expect she has a wardrobe full of umbrellas to match every outfit. After all, she is Queen of England!'

Whatever happens to the economy following the result of the EU referendum, umbrella manufacturers will continue to do well. It seems for us in these islands that global warming still produces rain, but now it is warm rain. And this is why we live in a green and pleasant land.

We enjoyed a rainy holiday in North Devon. One afternoon the characteristic summer weather provided a delightful insight into that type of character which is expressed in the saying, 'We are

British!' It was pouring down! Buckets of rain! Roads running with water! However, outside a small village hall was a weather-beaten notice, 'Cream teas today at 2:00 pm!' Drenched visitors were splashing through the puddles to enjoy the tea time treats, undaunted and undeterred by the circumstances around them. The Bible has this suitable verse: *'I have learned in whatever situation I am to be content.'* (Phil 4:11)

To be content with our circumstances does not mean we are complacent about them. We can 'Make the best of a bad job,'' but it is wiser to identify how we can make a bad job better. This is demonstrated by the way a Queen, wearing shocking pink, carried a shocking pink umbrella as a protection against a heavy grey sky. We noticed the colour of the umbrella rather than the ominous projection of the heavy clouds. Consider this line of a song, 'brighten the corner where you are.'

When we feel hemmed into a corner by adverse situations, we need to recollect that it is, after all, our corner and there is always a way to brighten it up! I had an Auntie who often said, 'Cheer up! It'll all be different in 100 years!' Undoubtedly true, but which of us still has 100 years? Remember: tomorrow is a new day. Jesus said, *'So do not worry about tomorrow; it will have enough worries of its own. There is no need to add to the troubles each day brings.'* (Matt 6:34) God's love is new every morning. Expect God to bless you - right now - and He will!

Strawberry Moon

In the fervor of the EU Referendum and the fragility of the situation following the result, maybe most of us missed the phenomenon of the strawberry moon, last seen on June 21st, 1967 and not visible again for another 46 years. The summer solstice and a full moon united in 2016 to present the longest day and the brightest night (cloud cover permitting). The title 'strawberry moon' was given by North American tribes who believed it heralded the beginning of the strawberry picking season! A rare fruit if picking it requires a 46 year wait! One newspaper in 2016 carried this beguiling headline: 'Summer ripens with strawberry moon on the shortest night.' Even though the full moon did not appear with a strawberry red surface, my attention was directed to the indisputable fact that we knew there would be a full moon on June 21st, 2016 and we also definitely anticipate another June 21st full moon in 46 years' time.

No one ever doubts the mathematical accuracy of the movements of sun, moon, stars, and planets. No one ever doubts gravity! One childish comment, following days of rain, was 'If the earth is round why doesn't the rain just fall off?' Gravity is infallible. When the astronaut returned from space, in the week of the strawberry moon, he was quoted as saying that he avoided looking out into space because there it was absolutely dark. Only earth carried light. This agrees with the Bible statement, *'In the beginning, when God created the universe, the earth was formless and desolate. The raging ocean that covered everything was engulfed in total darkness, and the Spirit of God was moving over the water. Then God commanded, "Let there be light"—and light appeared.'* (Gen 1:1–3)

Does anyone reading this ever doubt that tomorrow morning, it will be light? As with the predictable certainty of a strawberry moon on June 21st, 2016 so day always follows night, without a 46 year wait for the next dawn! The old adage, 'You can set your watch by it' is eternally true. The future, following the decision of the nation through the EU Referendum vote, is fraught, whatever politicians and pundits might affirm. Consider, then, these words from the Bible: *'The Lord's unfailing love and mercy still continue, Fresh as the morning, as sure as the sunrise. The Lord is all I have, and so in him I put my hope.'* (Lam 3:22–24)

Pretty Primroses

Have you seen these? A prettiness of primroses. A benediction of bluebells. A brilliance of buttercups. A delight of daisies. A marvel of May blossom. The extravagance of the displays at Chelsea flower show attain prime media coverage, but the shine of a hedgerow full of celandines is also worthy of multiple admiration, and we must never diminish the drama of dandelions, in full flower, on a motor way verge, even though we can classify all of them as a Wonder of Weeds! The Bible describes this treasure *'Consider the lilies, how they grow: they neither toil nor spin, yet I tell you, even Solomon in all his glory was not arrayed like one of these.'* (Luke 12:27) However - beauty is often in the eye of the beholder.

I recollect a true account which concerns an old lady, a group of clever crafts women, and a foreign potentate. Almost a century ago these ladies were asked to put together a gift of their best handiwork, which would be used to persuade a certain chief to allow a church and a hospital to be built on land which he owned.

The collection was amazingly beautiful, except for a patchwork quilt brought by an old lady who had heard about the venture. 'I made it with prayer,' she explained. However - the stitch work was clumsy (she had arthritic fingers) - the colors did not match (she had failing eye sight), and the leader of the group was inclined to 'lose' the quilt! Someone reminded her that there was a prayer in every stitch, so eventually, the quilt was used as a wrapper for the quality goods and duly dispatched across the oceans.

The haughty potentate regarded the carefully presented gifts with disdain. Then, his eye fell on the patchwork! He held it up, he gathered it around his shoulders, he held it up towards the strong tropical sun shine. 'This is a cloak fit for a king!' he said. In return for that quilt stitched together with prayer, he gave the land, and provided protection over the hospital when it was built. Beauty is in the eye of the beholder! And, yes—prayer always works wonders and brings blessing.

Lasting Memories

Holidays provide memories. I want to share an unusual one with you. At breakfast, in the hotel, the toast arrived, on a white china tray, ensconced in a white serviette to keep it warm! Ordinary brown bread thus acquired a new appearance which could enhance each slice and sandwich I eat in the future. Bread is the staff of life in western society. It is our basic food, which we take for granted, although local supermarkets stock an amazing variety of bread in a various shapes, sizes, and combination of ingredients.

When I was a little girl, Sunday tea always included a plate of brown bread, sliced thinly and with butter carefully spread from edge to crust-less edge. A feature in many restaurants is 'a bowl of soup with crusty, new baked bread.' Contrast a graceful cucumber sandwich with a chunky beef burger in an equally chunky roll. Do you remember having bread 'soldiers' to dip into a boiled egg? And if you are elderly, I guess you can remember the comfort provided by a bread poultice in those pre-antibiotic days? Can you recollect an occasion when bakers were on strike and for a short while there was no bread? That's when we suddenly realized how important it was to have bread and how necessary bread was as our staple diet.

We take so much for granted. Our country is at peace. No soldiers stalk our streets. Our children are educated and our elderly citizens receive pensions. The NHS ensures our well-being. Our shop shelves are full—we do not have to queue for our daily bread. We are free to worship God, no one prevents us from doing so. An old hymn admonishes us: *'Count your blessings, name them one by one, And it will surprise you what the Lord has done!'* (Hymn by Johnson Oatman Jr, 1897)

The Bible describes Jesus as the Bread of Life. One modern translation refers to him as *'An indispensable necessity, for everyday living.'* The availability of His presence, His protection, His peace and His providence has not diminished. He is the same - yesterday, today, and forever.

How is your appetite for the bread of life?

Live and Let Live

I once taught in a school in which 50% of the pupils were immigrants from Pakistan. We were a friendly, optimistic school and welcomed these children with interest and kindness. In classes of 30, they adapted to our language and habits; they were an asset to our school. The day came, however, when bureaucracy caught up with us!

The inspector in charge of 'racial integration' came to call. He required to speak to the whole school. He began, 'Now, who here knows they are different to the rest of you?' There were puzzled looks and silence. He persisted, 'Whose skin is a different colour?' Until then, no one in the entire group had taken any notice of skin colour. We were a happy and successful school and we accepted each other and worked together with harmony. We were red, black, white or any other rainbow shade!! The ensuing report decided that 'Further representation is not required.' That, of course, was then. In the 21st century, times have changed. But the question still needs to be answered - 'Who here is different to the rest?'

I was once visiting a patient in a psychiatric unit. Another patient was marching around, singing operatic arias in a loud tenor voice. One of the nurses explained his behavior: 'He wouldn't be in the hospital if he was in his own country,' she said. 'He just can't cope with the cold climate of the British Isles.' The Bible advises, *'Why, then, do you look at the speck in your brother's eye and pay no attention to the log in your own eye?'* (Matt 7:3)

We are all so individual that each of us has unique finger prints and a unique DNA. We should appreciate the differences of humankind and be excited by the variety of presentation and perception. Instead, we become fearful lest the routine of our tradition should be affected by different approaches to everyday living. We feel fraught in case the security of our society is disadvantaged by the addition of another culture. Dare we take the risk to live and let live? Our political leaders certainly need the help of our support and our prayers. And our children need the example of our courteous approach to strangers who come to live amongst us.

Consider this thought. *'Remember to welcome strangers in your homes. There were some who did that and welcomed angels without knowing it.'* (Heb 13:2)

Enjoy the Sunshine!

I read an account which identified that in the British Isles we need to take vitamin D supplement to ensure a healthy old age! This is due to a lack of sunshine, and a wide spread use of strong sun barrier creams. Advice was given; spend a short time each sunny day, in the sun, without sun cream. Children in particular need vitamin D to protect them from developing rickets. I appreciate this reminder of the blessing and benefit of sunshine, with the balance of good advice so that we are not injured by an excess of sun.

There is a balance to maintain in most situations. One of the major benefits in our society is that we are taught to read, and that there are plenty of things to read! Recently we visited Hay on Wye and we toured around the store which carries the title, 'The biggest second-hand book shop in the world!' It was an amazing experience, a real journey down memory lane on account of the generations of books on display and also a challenge to any reader thus confronted with all the books that are still there to be read. However, are books becoming out dated because we can now carry a complete library on our own mobile phone? Is this going to turn a town like Hay on Wye, into a large literature museum?

There needs to be a balance here, between the facility provided by IT and the printed, published presentation of thought, word, and deed available as a book. Surely discovering the expression of thought, word, and deed in a book cannot be compared to releasing the same experience by a click of a button?! It is rather like completely replacing summer sunshine with a tablet of vitamin D, there needs to be a balance between the two options. Consider these words from the Bible:

'The Preacher sought to find words of delight, and uprightly he wrote words of truth. ... The end of the matter; all has been heard. Fear God and keep his commandments, for this is the whole duty of man.' (from Eccl 12:10–13)

There is an old adage which advises: The best book to read is the Bible!

Enhance the Present

So far, the weather conditions this year have produced expansive growth. Our house has trees to the north, south, east and west - and recently the local council workforce came to trim certain trees, which were on their ground. The work was done with efficiency and courtesy and achieved an attractive solution to the tangle and overhang of the branches. The tree men created a new profile for each tree and thus the past was enhanced into the present.

We visited the Norwegian church in Cardiff Bay and the same thought crossed my mind; here, again, the past was enhanced into the present. This church was closed in 1974 but in 1987, it was dismantled and re-erected on its present site. Funded by money raised in both Wales and Norway, it is now an arts centre and a coffee shop. The descriptive brochure reads like this: 'The present use of the building recreates the tranquil, relaxed and welcoming character of the former church.' Surely this is an apt description of any church in which refreshment and the celebration of beauty are always part of worship and service. A church offers the unfailing sustenance of the Bread of Life and identifies the creative presence of God, who spoke everything into being. So, in the history of this church, indeed the past is enhanced into the present!

I thought of this when I visited an elderly friend in a residential home. The past seems finished—activity in business, work, home, social input—all restricted now by age and illness; but the kindness and care provided in the new residence can enhance the past into the present in quite a unique way. Elderly people deserve respect. They require to be treated with dignity. It is easy to forget the authority and ability which they used to display, when we are confronted with the ravages which many years of active life can bring. It is as if their tree of life has been trimmed into a new profile, or the body house in which they live has been dismantled and is now re-established on a different site. Support workers, staff in our residential homes, families—they all need our reassurance and understanding, and the support of our prayers. Consider this reminder from the Bible:

'And the King will answer them, 'Truly, I say to you, as you did it to one of the least of these my brothers, you did it to me.' (Matt 25:40)

Big Thoughts

Tourists were viewing Niagara Falls. One of them, a newly qualified plumber, surveyed the outrageous flow of water shrewdly. Then he turned to his companion and affirmed, 'You know, I could fix that!' Full marks for thinking big - but no marks for thinking he could control such power.

I was reminded of a small boy, busy with crayons and paper. Dad asked him, 'What are you drawing?' 'God,' was the simple answer. Dad said, 'How can you draw God? No one knows what He looks like.' His son replied, 'They will when I finish this - if I ever do.' He was thinking big about an infinite subject.

We live on a ball which we call planet Earth. It is immense in circumference, speeds around in space and its movements are so incredibly dependable so that, centuries ahead, its position in the universe can already be affirmed! But have you ever considered these facts and questioned why all the water doesn't just pour off this revolving planet of ours? Who has fixed it so that the water of Niagara doesn't plummet off into space?

We are so prone to take our 'plumbers kit' of human reasoning and fix away the grandeur and glory of God. We try to train the power of Niagara Falls to flow through the tap of what we can understand and control. We want to express God on the A4 page of our human intellect, in the colors of our own choice.

Maybe the tourist plumber had a second thought 'I'm glad that I don't have to fix it. I'll leave it to someone bigger than me.' Perhaps the junior artist finally realized that God is so big there is not enough paper or collection of colors in the world to really represent His presence. In which case, both of them were thinking big!

God is a big thinker. His big thought was to send Jesus - such an enormous thought, that even eternity will be too short to extol Him. Jesus came that we might be forgiven! He died to make us good. Now, we at last may go to Heaven, saved by his precious blood.

Blackberry Bushes

As I write, it is September. John Keats, in his poem 'To Autumn', described the month like this:

> *Season of mists and mellow fruitfulness,*
> *Close - bosomed friend of the maturing sun.*
> *Conspiring with him how to load and bless with fruit*
> *The vines that round the thatched eaves run.*

The blackberries are certainly large and luscious this year. The weather pattern has loaded the brambles and we can begin to enjoy the splendor of harvest.

In the late 19th century when whooping cough was prevalent, it was common to pass small children through a bramble bush as a cure. Once passed through the bush, an offering of bread and butter was left under the arch in the belief that the disease would leave with the food. In our century, whooping cough is almost eradicated. No one is likely to see a slice of bread and butter under a bramble bush, or a scratched but cured child skipping down the road. Times have changed! Some aspects of living do not change—autumn still produces its bounty of blackberries.

When Noah and his family came out of the ark, God said to them, *'As long as the earth endures, seedtime and harvest, cold and heat, summer and winter, day and night will never cease.'* The response, that some areas of planet earth are haunted by the prospect of famine, does not negate the promise. Maybe the operative phrase is 'as long as the earth endures'. Progress is rapid, food can be flown around the world in a matter of days—no country need starve, suffer deprivation, despair. The real truth is in the phrase 'only man is vile!'

Someone asked the question, 'Who is my neighbor?' We are all bound up in the bundle of life together, and my neighbor is anyone who breathes the air of our planet. September could be specially blessed, if each one of us took to heart the awareness that we should love our neighbor as ourselves.

Status Quo Vadis?

A late summer party in Hyde Park London featured Elton John and Status Quo and other more recent groups. A huge crowd of people celebrated and sang, but one of them related later that the most memorable moment for her was when one member of Status Quo said, 'Nowadays the stage is so full of cables that we have to be careful not to trip in case we can't get up again!'

It is always wise to watch where you put your feet. Consider the expression, 'Put your foot in it'. Frequently the media swoop on politicians who speak without careful thought, or forget to turn off their audio, or who speak without listening to advice. Advice in the Bible suggests 'in meekness of mind every man esteem others better than himself.' (Phil 2:3) When we think before we speak, and consider how other people might react to what we say, we are more likely to create a harmonious society and to protect peace. What used to be a spacious stage ready for the performers is now so full of microphones, loud speakers, audio equipment and cables that care is needed so that the show can go on—loudly—with all the entertainers on their feet! But we can't stop progress. Every aspect of living continues to develop and change. We have to accept change, even welcome it. After all, whoever objected to sliced bread?

Once we appreciated red kiosks and plumy voiced telephone operators; now we hold the world, via Google, in the palm of our hand. There are cars which do not need a driver. Robots are being developed to perform delicate eye surgery which human dexterity cannot manage.

What about the thought: 'To fall and not be able to rise again?' We all grow old—maybe we should use the phrase, we all mature! It is a privilege to attain 3 score years and ten, and then continue to add to that score. Many other members of the human race do not have the opportunity to live beyond 50 with the social problems they face. Our years give us a largesse of experience and memory, and when we have faith in God, every additional day is another day's march nearer our heavenly home. We know where we are going! So our response to Status Quo's comment should surely be, 'For what we have received, may the Lord make us truly thankful.'

> GOD,
> grant me the serenity
> to accept
> the things I cannot change;
> The courage
> to change
> the things I can;
> And the wisdom
> to know
> the difference.
>
> © Joyce Geleynse | Dreamstime.com

Prayer Works

Mosul – Aleppo – cities which are on the news most days, but which the majority of us will never visit. Cities which, if the news broadcasts are correct, will not be visitable in the future, even if we did try to go there. War is destroying them. One news reader said, 'Children here are terrified'. In our placid home in Wales we read, look and listen, and try not to entertain the thought, 'What if it happened here?'

I remember an incident some years ago, when the city of Sarajevo was in a similar precarious plight. I was with a group of 8-year-old children who were considering the situation. One said, 'What do the children do?' I replied, 'They stay hidden in places where bombs can't reach them. They don't go to school and they can't play outside'. Came the remark, 'So they don't play football and they stay inside even when the sun shines?' 'Yes,' I said. There was silence - then, 'Let's pray that today the children of Sarajevo can play out in the sunshine!' And that is what we did.

On the six o'clock news that evening, the announcer read: 'This has been a good day for the children of Sarajevo. Today, they have been able to play out in the sunshine. There had been an unexpected cease fire!' These were ordinary children who had an extra ordinary faith in the power of prayer. They prayed, with compassion for a situation which they could understand. Here were children who could not play outside, like they could - so they prayed that, somehow, the situation would be changed. And it was.

We can never dictate to God. We can never tell Him what to do. But we can ask Him to overrule and intervene into circumstances which are uncomfortable and hard, unjust and unlovely. We can petition Him on behalf of people who are in distress. When we can't cope, He can. Possibly one reason why the world is in such turmoil is because we do not pray. In our sophisticated society, we do not always include God in our activity. An old hymn uses these words: 'If our love were but more simple, we would take Him at His word. Then our lives would be all sunshine in the presence of the Lord.' So - what is His word? The Bible states, *'Pray without ceasing'*. (1 Thess 5:17 ESV)

Falling Leaves

There are more fallen leaves this year than there were last year—that is, if memory serves me right! Maybe the quantity of leaves in this autumn equates with the length and loveliness of summer days or the depth of snow in winter; distance lends enchantment, memory can exaggerate reality.

Is this why we can idealize those good old days? We forget how cold it was without central heating or how long the cold dark evenings were with only the light programme or the third programme for company - if we had remembered to get the accumulators charged, without which the radio could not even crackle. No TV then!

It is important that we remember with accuracy. When a person is brought to trial on evidence concerning an event which took place many years ago, how certain are they about what is said, on oath, to have taken place? We colour the past with the palette of the present. In a meeting the other day we were reminiscing about the 'good old days' when churches were full and every child went to Sunday school.

Now churches are poorly attended, many have closed down, very few children go to Sunday school. It seems that God has been forgotten, and social life has definitely not improved! Any TV programme or daily newspaper produces a sequence of avarice, greed, violence, cruelty pain, panic, political injustice which, to quote someone - 'Would make my Grandma blush!'

Everything is falling around us, like all these autumn leaves. The obvious thing to do with falling leaves is to sweep them up and get rid of them! Worship, praise and prayer are good sweeping brushes!

The Bible advises, *'Remember that there will be difficult times in the last days. ... But as for you, continue in the truths that you were taught. ... First of all, then, I urge that petitions, prayers, requests, and thanksgivings be offered to God for all people.'* (2 Tim 3:1, 14; 1 Tim 2:1)

The palette of this present does not enhance the past when, as a nation, we took time to remember God.

Battleship Banter!

I recollect the story of an unusual encounter at sea. A battle ship was coming in from maneuvers in heavy weather. Soon after darkness blackened the mist-filled sky, the look-out reported a light in the distance. The captain had this message sent: 'We are on a collision course. Please change your course 20 degrees'. A signal came back, 'More advisable for you to change your course.' The captain took umbrage. 'Send this signal,' he ordered. 'I am a captain! Change your course 20 degrees!' Back came the reply: 'I am a seaman, second class. But you had better change your course!' The captain barked a final threat 'I am in charge of a battle ship. Change your course!' This is the answer he received 'I am in charge of a lighthouse!'

We can go through life affirming our own progress. God signals, *'Trust in the Lord with all your heart, and do not lean on your own understanding.'* (Prov 3:5) God is light and He knows the way we should take. Amongst a welter of distressing news concerning the state of the world - war, destruction, famine, fear, violence—the item which was possibly the most threatening was the announcement that church attendance is declining and churches are closing! Without the light of places and people reserved and resolved for prayer, praise and worship, how can we avoid shipwreck on the sands of time?

The Bible reminds us that righteousness exalts a nation. Our streets and shops are already decked out for Christmas—some have been displaying glitter and sparkle since September! The excitement which characterizes Christmas sparkles everywhere, and certainly it should be gloriously presented, because Christmas is the time when we celebrate the occasion of God's personal entrance on planet earth.

Eventually the decorations will come down, BUT the light of the knowledge of the glory of God in the face of Jesus Christ continues for ever His presence is with us, 24/7. In the month of November, noted for remembrance, we could major on this fact. God promises to be with us always - even to the end of time itself.

The First Christmas

We have a delicate clump of primroses blooming on the edge of our lawn. The sky is grey and heavy with rain but they are as bright as if the only downpour was going to be a sweet April shower! The mountains are hidden in the mist, by 4:30 pm it will be dark BUT there are primroses defying the approach of the shortest, darkest day of the year—a visible announcement that if winter comes, then Spring cannot be far behind. Christmas coincides with the winter solstice, which is very appropriate because the Bible describes Jesus as the light of the world and light banishes darkness.

This is the story of the first Christmas. People were ordered by the government to return to their ancestral birth place, to be counted for taxing. Joseph and Mary were of the house and lineage of King David, so they set off for their ancestral home, Bethlehem. Mary was pregnant—without human intercourse—which no doubt caused tongues to wag in Nazareth where they were living. Maybe they travelled late to avoid curious eyes; whatever the reason, by the time they reached Bethlehem, there was no place for them in the inn. However, some kind innkeeper gave them the use of his stable; and that is where Jesus was born. Peaceful, private, and pleasant. A small haven of hope from the bustle, business, noise, festivity, delight of reunions, dancing, dogmatic debate (why should we pay taxes to Rome?) and discord. In the quiet stable, there was space for a delighted mother, and Joseph, to enjoy the new born baby.

Peace! Not the adjective best applied to Bethlehem at taxing time. The curt response 'No room in the inn for you!' is relevant for the crowds of refugees in our own time, pressing against the razor wire fences. There are people in our own town who feel left out through age, illness, family feuds, personal problems, forgotten faith; whatever the reason, they feel excluded from the easy greeting 'Happy Christmas!' The rising cost of postage is unfortunate, but a Christmas card from you to a neighbor or a friend might bring hope. I don't think you will find a card picturing primroses—but the effect of sending it might have the same effect as that little bunch of Spring on a winter lawn!

Happy Christmas Memories

Christmas is a season of happy memories. I recollect when a party of young people - I was young once! - were carol singing on a star spangled, frosty night, just before midnight, and we chose the carol 'Christians, awake!', at which, lights went on in bedroom windows, and we made a speedy retreat.

I recollect being on a late-night bus, and a group of workmen began to sing 'While shepherds watched their flocks by night', to the tune of 'Ilkley Moor'. They reached their stop before they reached the last verse, so the bus driver turned off the engine and we listened to those closing words:

All glory be to God on high, and to the earth be peace; Good will henceforth, from heaven to men, begin and never cease.

I recollect numerous nativity plays in schools, and the moments when the reality of the baby in the manger struck the children and their faces lit up with the recognition of the truth. But of all these delightful memories, I want to share with you an angel choir of six-year-old children, wearing wings and halos, balanced on a PE form, and singing lustily, 'The seven good joys that Mary had'.

Suddenly the PE form tipped over and all the angels fell onto the floor. But they did not stop singing! They picked themselves up, righted the form, and didn't miss a note! Because, of course, angels never stop singing.

This is so true. The Bible states that God *'will command his angels concerning you to guard you in all your ways'* (Ps 91:11 ESV). There are many of us who know that angels have been with us, often appearing in human guise, but always offering heavenly help.

Maybe the Christmas carol we should all adopt this Christmas is the one which contains these lines:

O hush the noise ye men of strife, and hear the angels sing!

Enjoy Today!

Memory can be elusive as we get older. When asked the date of his birthday, someone replied, 'I don't know when it happened but I know I have been born!' Actually, the date of Christmas could be said to match that statement. The church is not sure of the exact date of Jesus birth, approximately 2000 years ago, but history affirms that he was born, in Bethlehem. Initially, many different dates were considered, including January 2nd, March 21st, March 23rd, April 18th, April 19th, May 20th, May 28th, November 17th and November 20th!!

In the 4th century, the Western church decided to observe December 25th as Jesus birthday - and the eastern church followed suit. However, December 25th was also the date of several Roman holidays, celebrating the winter solstice, and worshipping the sun. Christian leaders did not think that matching the date in any way compromised their teaching with the culture, and responding to some criticism, a 4th century Bishop remarked, 'We hold that day holy, not like the pagans, because of the birth of the sun - but because of Him who made it.'

Whatever we might feel about the choice of December 25th as the date on which to celebrate Jesus birthday, we do know that it happened!

We could adapt a slogan and declare, 'Christ is not only for Christmas'. The Christian faith affirms that God is with us every day and a well-known carol contains these words, *'O holy child of Bethlehem, descend to us we pray. Cast out our sin and enter in: be born in us TODAY.'* (From 'O Little Town of Bethlehem' by Philip Brooks, 1867)

The Bible does not differentiate between months and seasons, but announces, *'This is the day that the Lord has made; let us rejoice and be glad in it' (Ps 118:24 ESV)* – glad in these 24 hours, this precious gift of time. The older we get, the more time seems to fly! I knew a lady who never took down her Christmas cards, because she said Christmas followed Christmas so quickly, it wasn't worth the trouble of unstringing them. Presumably, if a string broke, those cards were discarded, but certainly her house was always festooned with a multitude of Happy Christmas greetings. The only drawback, it seems to me, is that past greetings could obscure present greetings! Each today is God's Christmas gift to you and me.

Enjoy today!

Celebration Cake!

I once met a lady who told me an amazing story! She had saved ingredients from her meagre war-time rations to bake a celebration cake for when her son came home on his first leave from the Army.

The day came, and he arrived, accompanied by a troop of his friends! Undaunted, she handed out plates to everyone, produced the cake—baked in an 8-inch tin—and began to slice, and slice, and slice, enough for them all!

Now, how did that happen? Her explanation to me was that God always answers our prayers and meets our every need. She was a most matter of fact lady, not given to exaggeration, or even much conversation, but I recollect her final comment: "It was a miracle!"

How generous of God to bless her in this way. Generous is an appropriate adjective to apply to God, for He is indeed generous.

He has blessed us with another year, another 24 hours of life, a peaceful country—there is no war or famine here in Wales—and He hears our prayers and meets our needs when we ask for His help.

With the word "generous" still in mind, consider the generosity of the lady who received the miracle. She had saved from her own meagre rations a supply with which to bless someone else. When demand exceeded supply (more than 20 hungry men with an 8-inch cake!) she did not panic; instead she prayed.

As slice succeeded slice, she did not congratulate herself, she knew this was a gift from God, to enable her to bless her family and friends. She was not a headline lady, just a humble housewife with an unshakable faith in the God who cares.

Consider these lines from the Bible:

Trust in the Lord with all your heart. Never rely on what you think you know. Remember the Lord in everything you do, and he will show you the right way. (Prov 3:5–6)

He is the God who fed 5000 people with 5 loaves and 2 fish. Of course He could turn an 8-inch cake into a celebration feast!

What is your crisis today? What do you need? Our God is able to help!

More from Faithbuilders Publishing:

Faithbuilders Bible Study: The Gospel of Matthew

Faithbuilders Bible Study: The Gospel of Mark

The Pentecostal Bible Commentary Series: 1 Corinthians

The Prophet of Messiah

The Blessings of God's Grace

The Message of Mark

The Prophecy of Amos – A Warning for Today

More from Doreen Harrison

A Bouquet of Blessings

A Garland of Grace

Coping with the Wobbles of Life

The Donkey Boy

Jubilant Jeremy Johnson